O'Dwyer

by Iain Gray

LangSyne
PUBLISHING
WRITING *to* REMEMBER

Lang**Syne**

PUBLISHING

WRITING *to* REMEMBER

Vineyard Business Centre,
Pathhead, Midlothian EH37 5XP
Tel: 01875 321 203 Fax: 01875 321 233
E-mail: info@lang-syne.co.uk
www.langsyneshop.co.uk

Design by Dorothy Meikle
Printed by Ricoh Print Scotland
© Lang Syne Publishers Ltd 2011

ISBN 978-1-85217-409-5

O'Dwyer

MOTTO:
Virtue alone ennobles.

CREST:
A hand holding a sword.

NAME variations include:
Dwire
Dwier
Dwyer
Dyer
Mac Duibher *(Gaelic)*
Ó Dubhuir *(Gaelic)*
O'Duibhir *(Gaelic)*
Ó Duibhuir *(Gaelic)*

Chapter one:
Origins of Irish surnames

**According to an old saying, there are two types of Irish –
those who actually are Irish and those who wish they were.**

This sentiment is only one example of the allure that the
high romance and drama of the proud nation's history holds
for thousands of people scattered across the world today.

It's a sad fact, however, that the vast majority of Irish
surnames are found far beyond Irish shores, rather than on
the Emerald Isle itself.

The population stood at around eight million souls in
1841, but today it stands at fewer than six million.

This is mainly a tragic consequence of the potato
famine, also known as the Great Hunger, which devastated
Ireland between 1845 and 1849.

The Irish peasantry had become almost wholly reliant
for basic sustenance on the potato, first introduced from the
Americas in the seventeenth century.

When the crop was hit by a blight, at least 800,000
people starved to death while an estimated two million
others were forced to seek a new life far from their native
shores – particularly in America, Canada, and Australia.

The effects of the potato blight continued until about
1851, by which time a firm pattern of emigration had
become established.

Ireland's loss, however, was to the gain of the countries
in which the immigrants settled, contributing enormously,
as their descendants do today, to the well being of the
nations in which their forefathers settled.

But those who were forced through dire circumstance to
establish a new life in foreign parts never forgot their roots,
or the proud heritage and traditions of the land that gave
them birth.

Nor do their descendants.

It is a heritage that is inextricably bound up in the
colourful variety of Irish names themselves – and the origin
and history of these names forms an integral part of the
vibrant drama that is the nation's history, one of both
glorious fortune and tragic misfortune.

This history is well documented, and one of the most
important and fascinating of the earliest sources are *The
Annals of the Four Masters*, compiled between 1632 and
1636 by four friars at the Franciscan Monastery in County
Donegal.

Compiled from earlier sources, and purporting to go
back to the Biblical Deluge, much of the material takes in
the mythological origins and history of Ireland and the Irish.

This includes tales of successive waves of invaders and
settlers such as the Fomorians, the Partholonians, the
Nemedians, the Fir Bolgs, the Tuatha De Danann, and the
Laigain.

Of particular interest are the *Milesian Genealogies*,

because the majority of Irish clans today claim a descent from either Heremon, Ir, or Heber – three of the sons of Milesius, a king of what is now modern day Spain.

These sons invaded Ireland in the second millennium B.C, apparently in fulfilment of a mysterious prophecy received by their father.

This Milesian lineage is said to have ruled Ireland for nearly 3,000 years, until the island came under the sway of England's King Henry II in 1171 following what is known as the Cambro-Norman invasion.

This is an important date not only in Irish history in general, but for the effect the invasion subsequently had for Irish surnames.

'Cambro' comes from the Welsh, and 'Cambro-Norman' describes those Welsh knights of Norman origin who invaded Ireland.

But they were invaders who stayed, inter-marrying with the native Irish population and founding their own proud dynasties that bore Cambro-Norman names such as Archer, Barbour, Brannagh, Fitzgerald, Fitzgibbon, Fleming, Joyce, Plunkett, and Walsh – to name only a few.

These 'Cambro-Norman' surnames that still flourish throughout the world today form one of the three main categories in which Irish names can be placed – those of Gaelic-Irish, Cambro-Norman, and Anglo-Irish.

Previous to the Cambro-Norman invasion of the twelfth century, and throughout the earlier invasions and settlement of those wild bands of sea rovers known as the Vikings in the eighth and ninth centuries, the population of the island was relatively small, and it was normal for a person to be identified through the use of only a forename.

But as population gradually increased and there were many more people with the same forename, surnames were adopted to distinguish one person, or one community, from another.

Individuals identified themselves with their own particular tribe, or 'tuath', and this tribe – that also became known as a clann, or clan – took its name from some distinguished ancestor who had founded the clan.

The Gaelic-Irish form of the name Kelly, for example, is Ó Ceallaigh, or O'Kelly, indicating descent from an original 'Ceallaigh', with the 'O' denoting 'grandson of.' The name was later anglicised to Kelly.

The prefix 'Mac' or 'Mc', meanwhile, as with the clans of the Scottish Highlands, denotes 'son of.'

Although the Irish clans had much in common with their Scottish counterparts, one important difference lies in what are known as 'septs', or branches, of the clan.

Septs of Scottish clans were groups who often bore an entirely different name from the clan name but were under the clan's protection.

In Ireland, septs were groups that shared the same name and who could be found scattered throughout the four provinces of Ulster, Leinster, Munster, and Connacht.

The 'golden age' of the Gaelic-Irish clans, infused as their veins were with the blood of Celts, pre-dates the Viking invasions of the eighth and ninth centuries and the Norman invasion of the twelfth century, and the sacred heart of the country was the Hill of Tara, near the River Boyne, in County Meath.

Known in Gaelic as 'Teamhar na Rí', or Hill of Kings, it was the royal seat of the 'Ard Rí Éireann', or High King of Ireland, to whom the petty kings, or chieftains, from the island's provinces were ultimately subordinate.

It was on the Hill of Tara, beside a stone pillar known as the Irish 'Lia Fáil', or Stone of Destiny, that the High Kings were inaugurated and, according to legend, this stone would emit a piercing screech that could be heard all over Ireland when touched by the hand of the rightful king.

The Hill of Tara is today one of the island's main tourist attractions.

Opposition to English rule over Ireland, established in the wake of the Cambro-Norman invasion, broke out frequently and the harsh solution adopted by the powerful forces of the Crown was to forcibly evict the native Irish from their lands.

These lands were then granted to Protestant colonists, or 'planters', from Britain.

Many of these colonists, ironically, came from Scotland and were the descendants of the original 'Scotti', or 'Scots', who gave their name to Scotland after migrating there in the fifth century A.D., from the north of Ireland.

Colonisation entailed harsh penal laws being imposed on the majority of the native Irish population, stripping them practically of all of their rights.

The Crown's main bastion in Ireland was Dublin and its environs, known as the Pale, and it was the dispossessed peasantry who lived outside this Pale, desperately striving to eke out a meagre living.

It was this that gave rise to the modern-day expression of someone or something being 'beyond the pale'.

Attempts were made to stamp out all aspects of the ancient Gaelic-Irish culture, to the extent that even to bear a Gaelic-Irish name was to invite discrimination.

This is why many Gaelic-Irish names were anglicised with, for example, and noted above, Ó Ceallaigh, or O'Kelly, being anglicised to Kelly.

Succeeding centuries have seen strong revivals of Gaelic-Irish consciousness, however, and this has led to many families reverting back to the original form of their name, while the language itself is frequently found on the fluent tongues of an estimated 90,000 to 145,000 of the island's population.

Ireland's turbulent history of religious and political strife is one that lasted well into the twentieth century, a landmark century that saw the partition of the island into the twenty-six counties of the independent Republic of

Ireland, or Eire, and the six counties of Northern Ireland, or Ulster.

Dublin, originally founded by Vikings, is now a vibrant and truly cosmopolitan city while the proud city of Belfast is one of the jewels in the crown of Ulster.

It was Saint Patrick who first brought the light of Christianity to Ireland in the fifth century A.D.

Interpretations of this Christian message have varied over the centuries, often leading to bitter sectarian conflict – but the many intricately sculpted Celtic Crosses found all over the island are symbolic of a unity that crosses the sectarian divide.

It is an image that fuses the 'old gods' of the Celts with Christianity.

All the signs from the early years of this new millennium indicate that sectarian strife may soon become a thing of the past – with the Irish and their many kinsfolk across the world, be they Protestant or Catholic, finding common purpose in the rich tapestry of their shared heritage.

Chapter two:

Of royal race

Modern day County Tipperary, in the ancient southern province of Munster, was from earliest times the main territory of the O'Dwyers, although they were also to be found in significant numbers in the south of the eastern province of Leinster.

Original Gaelic forms of the name include Ó Duibhuir and Mac Duibher, indicating a descent from 'Duibhir', meaning 'black and dun coloured' – in all probability referring to Duibhir's hair colour.

In common with other native Irish clans that include those of Callaghan, Cassidy, Donnelly, Higgins, Kelly and O'Connor, the O'Dwyers and their namesakes the Dwyers can boast a truly royal pedigree.

This is through their descent from Heremon, one of the island's earliest monarchs.

Along with Heber, Ir, Amergin the Druid and four other brothers, he was a son of Milesius, a king of what is now modern day Spain, and who had planned to invade the Emerald Isle in fulfilment of a mysterious Druidic prophecy.

Milesius died before he could embark on the invasion but his sons, including Heremon, Heber, Ir and Amergin, successfully undertook the daunting task in his stead in about 1699 B.C.

Legend holds that their invasion fleet was scattered in a storm and Ir killed when his ship was driven onto the island of Scellig-Mhicheal, off the coast of modern day Co. Kerry.

Only Heremon, Heber and Amergin survived, although Ir left issue.

Heremon and Heber became the first of the Milesian monarchs of Ireland, but Heremon later killed Heber in a quarrel, while Amergin was slain by Heremon in an argument over territory.

The Co. Tipperary district of Kilnamagh became the main territory of the O'Dwyers.

This district, approximately one hundred square miles in area, is mute testimony to this day to the previous dominance of the O'Dwyers.

This is in the form of a number of ruined O'Dwyer castles that include those of Ballagh, Ballysheeda, Killenure and Milltown Castle – while the Dundrum House Hotel today sits on the site of what was Dundrum Castle.

Could the stones of these ruined castles speak, they would tell of centuries of both glorious fortune and tragic misfortune for the proud bearers of the O'Dwyer name.

It was following the late twelfth century Norman invasion of Ireland and the subsequent consolidation of the power of the English Crown that the ancient Gaelic way of life and power of the native Irish clans came under severe threat.

An indication of the harsh treatment meted out to them can be found in a desperate plea sent to Pope John XII by

Roderick O'Carroll of Ely, Donald O'Neil of Ulster and a number of other Irish chieftains in 1318.

They stated: 'As it very constantly happens, whenever an Englishman, by perfidy or craft, kills an Irishman, however noble, or however innocent, be he clergy or layman, there is no penalty or correction enforced against the person who may be guilty of such wicked murder.

'But rather the more eminent the person killed and the higher rank which he holds among his own people, so much more is the murderer honoured and rewarded by the English, and not merely by the people at large, but also by the religious and bishops of the English race.'

This appeal to the Pope had little effect on what became the increasingly harsh policy of the occupying English Crown against the native Irish such as the O'Dwyers.

Outbreaks of rebellion against the Crown were frequent and bloody, leaving large swathes of the island devastated and the haunt of carrion crows.

One particularly violent rebellion broke out in 1641 when landowners rebelled against the Crown's policy of settling, or 'planting' loyal Protestants on Irish land.

This policy had started during the reign from 1491 to 1547 of Henry VIII, whose Reformation effectively outlawed the established Roman Catholic faith throughout his dominions.

In the insurrection that exploded in 1641, at least 2,000

Protestant settlers were massacred, while thousands more were stripped of their belongings and driven from their lands to seek refuge where they could.

England had its own distractions with the Civil War that culminated in the execution of Charles I in 1649, and from 1641 to 1649 Ireland was ruled by a rebel group known as the Irish Catholic Confederation, or the Confederation of Kilkenny.

One of the leading rebels was Philip O'Dwyer, Chief of the Clan, who had led his kinsfolk on a successful assault of the forbidding bastion of the Rock of Cashel in 1641, routing its defenders and occupying it in their place.

A rocky plateau that rises about 300ft above the plain known as the Golden Valley of Tipperary, the Rock of Cashel – with 'cashel' derived from the Gaelic 'caiseal', meaning 'stone fort' – had been fortified since as early as the fourth century.

It was here that St Patrick is reputed to have converted Aengus Mac Mutfraich, a king of Munster, to Christianity, while it was also the seat for a time of the great early eleventh century High King, Brian Boru.

Philip O'Dwyer, the last of the O'Dwyer Chiefs, died in 1648, but his rebel force held out on the Rock of Cashel until it was stormed and taken by a Cromwellian force under the command of Murrough O'Brien.

The English Civil War had intervened to prevent immediate action against Confederate Ireland, but following the execution of Charles I and the consolidation of the power of England's Oliver Cromwell, the time was ripe was revenge.

Cromwell descended on Ireland at the head of a 20,000-strong army that landed at Ringford, near Dublin, in August of 1649.

He had three main aims: to quash all forms of rebellion, to 'remove' all Catholic landowners who had taken part in the rebellion, and to convert the native Irish to the Protestant faith.

An early warning of the terrors that were in store for the native Irish came when the northeastern town of Drogheda was stormed and taken in September and between 2,000 and 4,000 of its inhabitants killed.

The defenders of Drogheda's St. Peter's Church, who had refused to surrender, were burned to death as they huddled for refuge in the steeple and the church was deliberately torched.

Word of the slaughter at Drogheda had already reached the inhabitants of the town of Cashel and, fearing a similar fate, large numbers of the townsfolk and rebel soldiers sought refuge in the church.

Ignoring the sanctity of this refuge, Murrough O'Brien's troopers stacked piles of turf around its walls and, setting them alight, left the hapless occupants of the church to slowly roast to death.

The leader of the rebel forces in Munster was Colonel

Edmund O'Dwyer, who finally surrendered to the Cromwellian forces at Cahir, Co. Tipperary, in 1652.

Cromwell soon held the benighted land in a grip of iron, allowing him to implement what amounted to a policy of ethnic cleansing.

His troopers were given free rein to hunt down and kill priests, while rebel estates were confiscated, including those of the O'Dwyers.

An estimated 11 million acres of land were confiscated and the dispossessed Irish banished to Connacht and Co. Clare, while an edict was issued stating that any native Irish found east of the River Shannon after May 1, 1654, faced either summary execution or transportation to the West Indies.

Colonel O'Dwyer and many of his kinsfolk were among the hundreds of Irish who were exiled to the Continent, where they managed to forge new lives for themselves – although in later centuries many O'Dwyers returned to their original heartland of Co. Tipperary.

Chapter three:
United Irishmen

Rebellion erupted again nearly 150 years later in the form of the Rising of 1798, aimed at restoring Irish freedom and independence from English rule.

The roots of the Rising are tangled in the thick undergrowth of Irish history, but in essence it was sparked off by a fusion of sectarian and agrarian unrest and a burning desire for political reform that had been shaped by the French revolutionary slogan of 'liberty, equality and fraternity.'

A movement had come into existence that embraced middle-class intellectuals and the oppressed peasantry, and if this loosely bound movement could be said to have had a leader, it was Wolfe Tone, a Protestant from Kildare and leading light of a radical Republican movement known as the United Irishmen.

Despite attempts by the British government to concede a degree of agrarian and political reform, it was a case of far too little and much too late, and by 1795 the United Irishmen, through Wolfe Tone, were receiving help from France – Britain's enemy.

A French invasion fleet was despatched to Ireland in December of 1796, but it was scattered by storms off Bantry Bay.

Two years later, in the summer of 1798, rebellion broke out on the island.

The first flames of revolt were fanned in Ulster, but soon died out, only to be replaced by a much more serious conflagration centred mainly in Co. Wexford.

Victory was achieved at the battle of Oulart Hill, followed by another victory at the battle of Three Rocks, but the peasant army was no match for the 20,000 troops or so that descended on Wexford.

Defeat followed at the battle of Vinegar Hill on 21 June, followed by another decisive defeat at Kilcumney Hill five days later.

One of the leading rebels was Michael Dwyer, born in 1772 in Co. Wicklow, and who was better known as The Wicklow Chief. A member of the Society of United Irishmen, he fought in engagements that included Vinegar Hill and, undaunted by the failure of the Rising, continued to wage a campaign of guerrilla warfare against the forces of the Crown throughout Wicklow until as late as 1803.

Wicklow became the last bastion of the rebels and thousands of troops were deployed to run The Wicklow Chief to ground.

He narrowly evaded capture in December of 1799 when a cottage in which he was sheltering at Derrynamuck was surrounded and attacked: a blazing gun battle ensued, and O'Dwyer managed to escape in the confusion after the cottage caught fire.

The increasingly frustrated authorities, desperate to capture Dwyer, offered a large reward for information leading to his whereabouts, while anyone known to have provided him with shelter incurred harsh punishment.

Finally offered terms that would allow him to leave Ireland for America, he surrendered in December of 1803.

But the authorities reneged on the deal and imprisoned him for nearly two years in Dublin's Kilmainham Prison, before transporting him as "an unsentenced exile" to New South Wales – where even further trials and tribulations awaited him.

Accompanied by his wife and two eldest children, he was granted land at Cabramatta Creek, Sydney, but it was not long before the bold Dwyer incurred the wrath of the British colonial authorities.

Reported to have boasted that "all Irish will be free in this new country", he was arrested and charged in May of 1807 with conspiring to mount an insurrection against British rule.

At the subsequent trial, he was found not guilty but, ignoring this, Governor William Bligh put him on trial again.

Found guilty this time, he was stripped of his free settler status and transported to Van Diemens Land, now Tasmania.

Less than a year later, however, a new governor

overturned the guilty verdict and reinstated Dwyer's free settler status.

With a fine touch of irony, the former rebel rose to serve as Chief of Police of Sydney, serving from 1813 until 1820, when he was dismissed for drunken misconduct and the mislaying of important police documents.

Bankrupted and forced to sell his farm two years later, he was imprisoned for a time in Sydney's debtors' prison, where he contracted the dysentery that eventually put an end to his life in August of 1825.

His remains now lie in Sydney's Waverley Cemetery, where a monument to the famed Wicklow Chief was erected in 1900.

Dwyer left seven children and, in 2002, at Bungendore, near Canberra, a number of his descendants met for a family reunion.

One particularly controversial bearer of the O'Dwyer name was Sir Michael O'Dwyer, who was born in the original O'Dwyer heartland of Co.Tipperary in 1864 and who fell victim to an assassin's bullet in 1940.

Appointed Lieutenant Governor of the Punjub, India, in 1912, it was in April of 1919 that riots broke out after he wielded his authority to expel two popular Indian nationalists from Amritsar.

Public buildings were looted and burned and five Englishmen murdered.

O'Dwyer imposed martial law, and it was in this

extremely volatile atmosphere that a large crowd of Indians gathered on April 13 at the Jallianwala Bagh stadium in Amritsar.

The crowd was faced by a number of Gurkha troops under the nervous command of Brigadier General Reginald Dyer, who ordered his troops to open fire.

At least 379 unarmed civilians were killed in the ensuing mayhem, although some sources place a much higher figure on the number of victims.

International outrage followed the massacre, with O'Dwyer becoming the centre of controversy for his apparent support of the action taken by Brigadier General Dyer.

Twenty-one years later, in March of 1940, he was attending a meeting of the Royal Central Asian Society in Caxton Hall, London, when he was shot and killed in revenge for the massacre by the Punjabi revolutionary Udham Singh.

Seven years before his murder, and much less controversially, O'Dwyer published a detailed and invaluable history of the O'Dwyers – *The O'Dwyers of Kilnamanagh: The History of an Irish Sept*, re-published in recent years as *The History of the O'Dwyers*.

Bearers of the O'Dwyer name in its equally popular spelling variant of Dwyer fought bravely in different fields of conflict. Edward Dwyer, born in 1895 in Fulham, London was a First World War recipient of the Victoria

Cross (V.C.), the highest award for bravery in the face of enemy action for British and Commonwealth forces.

He had been a private in the 1st Battalion, East Surrey Regiment, when, in April of 1915 at Hill 60, in Belgium, while his trench was under heavy attack, he managed to disperse the enemy by climbing on the parapet and attacking them with hand grenades.

Later promoted to corporal, he was killed in action just over a year later.

Yet another First World War recipient of the V.C. was John Dwyer, born in 1890 in Port Cygnet, Tasmania, and later a noted Australian politician.

He had been a sergeant in the 4th Company, Machine Gun Corps, Australian Imperial Force, when, in September of 1917 at Zonnebeke, Belgium, he single-handedly rushed his machine gun forward to within 30 yards of German lines and killed a machine gun crew.

Later promoted to lieutenant, he entered politics after the war and served as First Deputy Premier of his native Tasmania from 1958 until 1959; he died in 1962.

Chapter four:

On the world stage

Bearers of the O'Dwyer and Dwyer names have found fame through a rich variety of endeavours and pursuits.

Best known for her roles in a number of British horror films of the late 1960s and early 1970s, **Hilary Dwyer** is the actress and film producer born in 1945 in Liverpool.

Her horror film roles include the 1968 *Witchfinder General*, the 1969 *The Oblong Box* and, from 1970, *Cry of the Banshee*.

Television roles include the cult classic *The Prisoner*, while it is under her married name of Hilary Heath that she now enjoys a career as a producer, responsible for television productions that include the 1998 *Criminal Law* series.

Appearing in British television classics that include episodes of *Z-Cars*, *The Sweeney* and the sitcom *Hi-de-Hi!* **Leslie Dwyer** was the actor who was born in 1906 in Catford, London. The actor, who died in 1986, also had roles in a number of films that include the 1942 *In Which We Serve*, the 1959 remake of director Alfred Hitchcock's *The 39 Steps* and, from 1966, *Die, Monster, Die!*

Born in 1973 in Syston, Leicestershire, **Terri Dwyer** is the actress who has appeared in popular British television programmes that include *Grange Hill*, *Hollyoaks* and *Loose Women*.

Also in television, **Declan O'Dwyer**, born in 1968, is the Irish director who has worked on a number of British productions that include *Casualty*, *The Bill* and *Wire in the Blood*, while he is also a member of the Directors Guild of Great Britain.

Across the Atlantic, **Bil Dwyer**, born in 1962 in Evergreen Park, Illinois, is the popular American television game show host and stand-up comedian who has hosted shows that include *Extreme Dodgeball* and *I've Got a Secret*.

Behind the camera lens, **Michael Dwyer** was the highly respected Irish film critic who was born in 1951 in Tralee, Co. Kerry, and who died in 2010.

In addition to writing for the *Irish Times* for more than 20 years, he was a co-founder of the Dublin Film Festival and, in 2002, the Dublin International Film Festival, and served on the board of the Irish Museum of Modern Art.

Bearers of the O'Dwyer and Dwyer names have also excelled, and continue to excel, in the highly competitive world of sport.

On the fields of Gaelic football, **Mick O'Dwyer** is the manager and former skilled forward hailed as one of the sport's most successful managers of all time.

This accolade was bestowed with respect to his management from 1974 to 1989 of the Kerry senior football team.

Born in 1936 in Waterville, Co. Kerry, and a player

for Waterville from 1953 to 1984, he is also the holder of four All-Ireland titles and eleven Munster inter-county titles.

A member from 1995 until 2005 of the Cork senior inter-county team, **Kevin O'Dwyer** is the retired Gaelic football goalkeeper, born in 1973 in Skibbereen, Co. Cork, and whose local club was O'Donovan Rossa.

Also in Ireland, and in the equally popular sport of hurling, **Noel O'Dwyer**, born in 1949 in Borrisoleigh, in the ancient O'Dwyer heartland of Co. Tipperary, is the retired player whose local club was Borris-Ileigh and who was a member in the 1960s and later in the 1980s of the Tipperary senior inter-county team.

In the Irish sport of camogie, **Una O'Dwyer**, born in 1982 in Tipperary, is the player who won both the 2004 Texaco Player of the Year Award and the All-Star Award, and whose local club is Cashel and County.

In the saddle, **Martin Dwyer**, born in 1975 in Aintree, Merseyside, is the English flat racing jockey who won the Epsom Oaks in 2003, riding Casual Look and the 2006 Derby on Sir Percy.

Across the Atlantic to the sport of ice hockey, **Billy O'Dwyer** is the retired American professional forward, born in 1960 in Boston, who played for teams that include the Los Angeles Kings and the Boston Bruins.

Born in 1978 in Dalhousie, New Brunswick, **Gordie Dwyer** is the Canadian who has played ice hockey for teams that include Tampa Bay Lightning, Montreal Canadiens and the New York Rangers.

In field hockey, **Jamie Dwyer**, born in 1979 in Rockhampton, Queensland, is the striker who captained Australia to victory in the final of the 2010 Hockey World Cup and who was also a member of the team that won the gold medal at the 2004 Olympics.

On the fields of European football, **Phil Dwyer** is the Welsh former player who earned ten caps playing for his home country between 1978 and 1979.

Born in Cardiff in 1953, he played club football for Cardiff City between 1972 and 1985.

In American football, **Matt O'Dwyer**, born in 1972 in Lincolnshire, Illinois, is the former football guard who played for teams that include the New York Jets, Cincinnati Bengals and, in 2004, the Tampa Bay Buccaneers.

On the cricket pitch, **Edmund O'Dwyer**, born in 1919 in Bridgetown, Western Australia, and who died in 2005, was the left arm batsman and bowler who has the distinction of having been the last player to dismiss the great Don Bradman in a first class match.

From the competitive world of sport to the equally competitive and often cut-throat world of politics, **William O'Dwyer** and his younger brother **Paul O'Dwyer** found new lives for themselves on foreign shores – not only to the benefit of themselves but to that of the nation in which they settled.

Born in Co. Mayo in 1894, one of eleven siblings, he

abandoned his studies in Ireland to become a priest and immigrated to the United States.

Working for a time as a labourer, he later joined the ranks of the New York City Police Department while burning the midnight oil to study law.

Qualifying as a lawyer in 1923, he went on to establish a successful legal practice and later serve as a court judge in Brooklyn.

Elected as a district attorney for King's County District, New York, in 1939, he gained national fame through his prosecution of the notorious crime syndicate, Murder Inc., while he later served, from 1946 to 1950, as the 100th Mayor of New York.

It was in recognition of his outstanding contribution to the City of New York that in 1948 he received The Hundred Year Association of New York's Gold Medal Award.

He died in 1964, survived by his brother Paul, who had also settled in New York.

Born in 1907, he not only followed in his brother's footsteps as a lawyer, but also became a noted defender of civil rights and a highly vocal opponent of the Vietnam War.

Serving on the board of America's National Lawyers Guild from 1948 to 1951, he also served from 1974 to 1977 as president of New York City Council.

The lawyer and politician also won the Democratic primary for U.S. Senator for New York State in 1968, but lost to his Republican Party opponent; he died in 1998, aged 91.

In Australia, John Patrick Dwyer, better known as **Jack Dwyer**, born in 1879 in Aberfeldy, Victoria, and who died in 1966, served as Chief Justice and Lieutenant Governor of the State of Western Australia from 1949 to 1959.

Also in Australia, **Kate Dwyer** was a leading labour activist and suffragist.

Born in 1861 in Tambaroora, New South Wales, she was a founder in 1901of the Women's Progressive Association, Australia, that fought for equal benefits for women and for their entry into the legal profession.

Also the founder of the Women Workers' Union, in 1921 she became the first female Justice of the Peace to be appointed in New South Wales; she died in 1949.

In the creative world of contemporary art, **Sean O'Dwyer** is the Irish painter and sculptor whose impressive four-metre tall granite sculpture, *Ready Boat Pillar*, was unveiled in 1996 in the fishing village of Howth, Co. Dublin.

O'Dwyer, who was born in 1964 in Nenagh, Co. Tipperary, in 2007 unveiled his painting *The Miracle Ship* – based on a curious folk legend that, during the Great Famine of the nineteenth century, aid was brought to the citizens of the east coast town of Drogheda by a Turkish ship from the Ottoman Empire.

To art of a much different genre, **Kieron Dwyer**, born in 1967, is the acclaimed American comic book artist best known for his work on *Action Comics* in the mid-1990s, and the *Captain America* and *Danger Unlimited* series.

In the field of medicine, **Joseph O'Dwyer**, born in 1841 in Cleveland, Ohio, left an enduring legacy through his invention of the medical technique known as intubation – where a tube is utilised to open the larynx.

Graduating from the College of Physicians of New York in 1865 and later appointed to the medical staff of the New York Foundling Asylum, he first developed his intubation technique to avoid death by suffocation of children struck with diphtheria.

He died in 1898, but his technique is still in use throughout the world today, and is responsible for saving thousands of lives annually.

Also remembered to this day, but for decidedly different reasons than Joseph O'Dwyer, is the notorious American bootlegger William Vincent Dwyer, better known as **Big Bill Dwyer**.

Born in what was the notorious Hell's Kitchen district of Manhattan in 1883, he set up as a bootlegger during the Prohibition era of the 1920s – accumulating enough from his ill-gotten gains to buy a number of prestigious sporting enterprises that included the Brooklyn Dodgers of the National Football League.

Responsible for an operation that smuggled alcohol from Europe directly to New York, the former dock worker managed to evade the forces of the law until as late as 1935 – when a lawsuit brought against him by the U.S. Government stripped him of his fortune; he died in 1946.

Key dates in Ireland's history from the first settlers to the formation of the Irish Republic:

circa 7000 B.C.	Arrival and settlement of Stone Age people.
circa 3000 B.C.	Arrival of settlers of New Stone Age period.
circa 600 B.C.	First arrival of the Celts.
200 A.D.	Establishment of Hill of Tara, Co. Meath, as seat of the High Kings.
circa 432 A.D.	Christian mission of St. Patrick.
800-920 A.D.	Invasion and subsequent settlement of Vikings.
1002 A.D.	Brian Boru recognised as High King.
1014	Brian Boru killed at battle of Clontarf.
1169-1170	Cambro-Norman invasion of the island.
1171	Henry II claims Ireland for the English Crown.
1366	Statutes of Kilkenny ban marriage between native Irish and English.
1529-1536	England's Henry VIII embarks on religious Reformation.
1536	Earl of Kildare rebels against the Crown.
1541	Henry VIII declared King of Ireland.
1558	Accession to English throne of Elizabeth I.
1565	Battle of Affane.
1569-1573	First Desmond Rebellion.
1579-1583	Second Desmond Rebellion.
1594-1603	Nine Years War.
1606	Plantation' of Scottish and English settlers.
1607	Flight of the Earls.
1632-1636	Annals of the Four Masters compiled.
1641	Rebellion over policy of plantation and other grievances.
1649	Beginning of Cromwellian conquest.
1688	Flight into exile in France of Catholic Stuart monarch James II as Protestant Prince William of Orange invited to take throne of England along with his wife, Mary.
1689	William and Mary enthroned as joint monarchs; siege of Derry.
1690	Jacobite forces of James defeated by William at battle of the Boyne (July) and Dublin taken.

1691	Athlone taken by William; Jacobite defeats follow at Aughrim, Galway, and Limerick; conflict ends with Treaty of Limerick (October) and Irish officers allowed to leave for France.
1695	Penal laws introduced to restrict rights of Catholics; banishment of Catholic clergy.
1704	Laws introduced constricting rights of Catholics in landholding and public office.
1728	Franchise removed from Catholics.
1791	Foundation of United Irishmen republican movement.
1796	French invasion force lands in Bantry Bay.
1798	Defeat of Rising in Wexford and death of United Irishmen leaders Wolfe Tone and Lord Edward Fitzgerald.
1800	Act of Union between England and Ireland.
1803	Dublin Rising under Robert Emmet.
1829	Catholics allowed to sit in Parliament.
1845-1849	The Great Hunger: thousands starve to death as potato crop fails and thousands more emigrate.
1856	Phoenix Society founded.
1858	Irish Republican Brotherhood established.
1873	Foundation of Home Rule League.
1893	Foundation of Gaelic League.
1904	Foundation of Irish Reform Association.
1913	Dublin strikes and lockout.
1916	Easter Rising in Dublin and proclamation of an Irish Republic.
1917	Irish Parliament formed after Sinn Fein election victory.
1919-1921	War between Irish Republican Army and British Army.
1922	Irish Free State founded, while six northern counties remain part of United Kingdom as Northern Ireland, or Ulster; civil war up until 1923 between rival republican groups.
1949	Foundation of Irish Republic after all remaining constitutional links with Britain are severed.